CONTENDING
FOR THE
Faith

CONTENDING FOR THE

THE STORY OF THE WESTMINSTER ASSEMBLY

Joel R. Beeke and William Boekestein

Reformation Heritage Books
Grand Rapids, Michigan

Contending for the Faith
© 2022 by Joel R. Beeke and William Boekestein

All rights reserved. No part of this book may be used or reproduced in any manner whatsoever without written permission except in the case of brief quotations embodied in critical articles and reviews. Direct your requests to the publisher at the following addresses:

Reformation Heritage Books
3070 29th St. SE
Grand Rapids, MI 49512
616-977-0889
orders@heritagebooks.org
www.heritagebooks.org

Printed in the United States of America
22 23 24 25 26 27/10 9 8 7 6 5 4 3 2 1

Scripture taken from the King James Version. In the public domain.

Library of Congress Cataloging-in-Publication Data

Names: Beeke, Joel R., 1952- author. | Boekestein, William, author.
Title: Contending for the faith : the story of the Westminster Assembly / Joel R. Beeke and William Boekestein.
Description: Grand Rapids, Michigan : Reformation Heritage Books, [2022] | Audience: Ages 7–12
Identifiers: LCCN 2021042227 | ISBN 9781601789181 (hardcover)
Subjects: LCSH: Westminster Assembly (1643-1652)—Juvenile literature.
Classification: LCC BX9053 .B38 2022 | DDC 262/.55—dc23
LC record available at https://lccn.loc.gov/2021042227

For additional Reformed literature, request a free book list from Reformation Heritage Books at the above regular or email address.

The authors wish to thank Paul Smalley and Ray Lanning for their invaluable assistance in editing and finalizing this book.

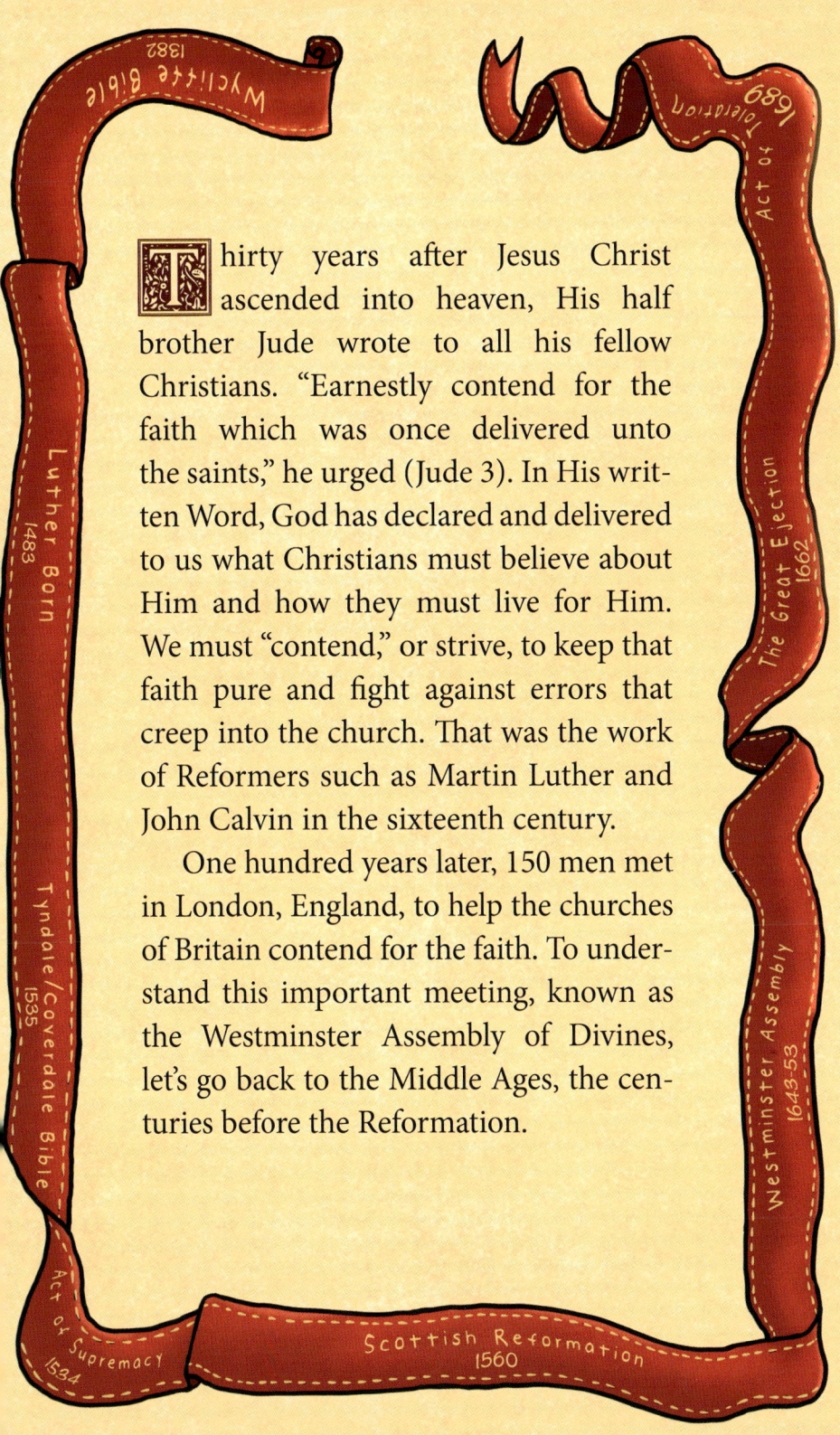

Thirty years after Jesus Christ ascended into heaven, His half brother Jude wrote to all his fellow Christians. "Earnestly contend for the faith which was once delivered unto the saints," he urged (Jude 3). In His written Word, God has declared and delivered to us what Christians must believe about Him and how they must live for Him. We must "contend," or strive, to keep that faith pure and fight against errors that creep into the church. That was the work of Reformers such as Martin Luther and John Calvin in the sixteenth century.

One hundred years later, 150 men met in London, England, to help the churches of Britain contend for the faith. To understand this important meeting, known as the Westminster Assembly of Divines, let's go back to the Middle Ages, the centuries before the Reformation.

Two hundred years before the Reformation, John Wycliffe worked hard to make it possible for English Christians to read God's Word in their own language. Toward that end, he published the first English translation of the Holy Scriptures, which he and his helpers translated from the Latin Bible.

By the time the ideas of the Reformation came to England, Wycliffe's Bible had given place to other translations. In 1525 William Tyndale published an English translation of the Greek New Testament. Though Tyndale was put to death for his faith, Myles Coverdale published a complete English Bible in 1535, using much of Tyndale's work. Englishmen could read the Bible in their own language and began to question the teachings and worship of the Roman Catholic Church, which everyone belonged to in those days.

The English Reformation began in a way you might not have expected. In 1534 King Henry VIII forced Parliament, the lawmakers of England, to pass the Act of Supremacy. The king was proclaimed Supreme Governor of the Church of England. Henry made this decision for personal reasons. He wanted to divorce his wife, who had not given him a son. The pope, the head of the Roman Catholic Church, refused. So Henry announced that the pope was no longer head of the English Church. But at the same time, a new law required all Englishmen to agree with Roman Catholic doctrines about the seven sacraments, priests not getting married, and confessing their sins to a priest. Henry wasn't interested in a true reformation. But he had opened the door for big changes in the church.

After Henry's death, his son, Edward, became king at age nine. Edward's counselors helped him reform the English Church according to Scripture. He outlawed the worship of images. Priests no longer had to remain unmarried. Thomas Cranmer's Book of Common Prayer (1549) provided a complete form of worship in English. Scotsman John Knox and others summarized the church's faith in a creed called the Forty-Two Articles of Religion (1552). The Reformation was going well—until Edward suddenly died at the age of fifteen.

The new queen was Edward's half sister Mary, who hated the changes that her father and brother had begun to make in the church. She undid all their work and brought the church back under the headship of the Roman Catholic pope. "Bloody Mary" and her husband, Philip of Spain, mercilessly persecuted those who favored reformation. Many Christian leaders fled to the European mainland, and especially to Geneva in Switzerland.

In 1558 Mary died, and her half sister, Elizabeth, became queen. Elizabeth was not Roman Catholic and returned England to the Reformed faith. The Book of Common Prayer and the Thirty-Nine Articles of Religion (based on the Forty-Two Articles) controlled the worship and doctrine of the Church of England. But Elizabeth retained some pre-Reformation customs in public worship. She wanted to find a "middle way" between the warring factions of her national church.

Some Christians wanted to bring the work and worship of their church into closer conformity to the Bible, in all it teaches and commands. They believed the Church of England should be more like Reformed churches in Scotland, the Netherlands, and Switzerland. They called for more preaching of God's Word and less ceremonialism, so that people would learn to trust in Christ alone and serve God from the heart. These Christians were nicknamed Puritans by people who did not like them.

When Elizabeth died in 1603, her throne passed to James, king of Scotland. King James ruled over the three kingdoms of England, Scotland, and Ireland. Though raised in the Reformed faith, James warmly endorsed Elizabeth's policy regarding the national church. He was a huge disappointment to the Puritans and threatened to "harry them out of this land."

Under the next king, Charles, the conflict deepened. King Charles's top churchman, Archbishop Laud, punished Puritans severely when they did not conform to his dictates. But when Laud tried to force the Scottish church

to be like the Church of England, Scottish Christians rebelled. They entered into a National Covenant to defend the faith and practice of the Reformed Church of Scotland. Charles called Parliament in 1640 to raise money for an army to crush the Scottish Covenanters. To Charles's horror, Parliament instead put Laud in prison on a charge of treason.

Soon two armies, one loyal to the king and the other to Parliament—led by commanders such as Oliver Cromwell—began a civil war.

In late 1641, Parliament sent King Charles a Grand Remonstrance that asked him to make changes in his rule over church and state. In it, they also asked for him to call an assembly of the best divines, or gospel ministers, of the nation to give advice to Parliament for the peace and good government of the church. Charles refused.

Finally, in June 1643, in the midst of the civil war, Parliament itself called such an assembly. It would consist of 30 members of Parliament (10 from the House of Lords and 20 from the House of Commons) and 121 ministers from every county of the kingdom. They assembled in Westminster Abbey, a large building in London where British kings and queens are traditionally crowned, near the place where Parliament meets.

The Westminster Assembly included many of the brightest minds and godliest men of the day, such as William Gouge, Thomas Gataker, and Anthony Burgess. William Greenhill, Jeremiah Burroughs, William Bridge, and Thomas Goodwin had earlier been forced to flee to the Netherlands to escape persecution. Goodwin and Edward Reynolds were later given important posts at Oxford University, and Anthony Tuckney at Cambridge University. John Wallis was not only a theologian but a great mathematician.

The Scottish commissioners were fewer in number but extremely helpful. Alexander Henderson was masterful in both doctrine and diplomacy. Robert Baillie left a careful record of the Assembly in his letters and journals. Samuel Rutherford's devotion to Christ and grasp of theology are well known. The young George Gillespie had skill in debating far beyond his years.

On July 1, 1643, in the Chapel of Henry VII at Westminster Abbey, the chairman, William Twisse, gave the opening sermon on John 14:18. Most of the later meetings were held in the Abbey's Jerusalem Chamber, which had fireplaces to keep the members warm. Members of Parliament were privileged to sit by the fireplaces.

For nearly six years, the Assembly met Monday through Friday, usually from morning until afternoon. Every session began and ended with prayer. Every Monday morning each member—there were usually sixty to eighty at the meetings—renewed his vow, "in the presence of Almighty God, that in this Assembly, whereof I am a member, I will maintain nothing in point of doctrine, but what I believe to be most agreeable to the word of God; nor in point of discipline, but what may make most for God's glory, and the peace and good of this church." Fast days for God's guidance were also often appointed, which included sermons and prayers that could last all day.

Parliament had called the Assembly to give advice on "a further and more perfect reformation" of the Church of England by God's Word.

The Assembly began to revise the Thirty-Nine Articles of Religion. That work ended when Parliament sent men to Scotland to plead for help in the war with King Charles. The Scots wanted the English to commit to a Reformed church in all three kingdoms, and so they entered into the Solemn League and Covenant of 1648.

Under this agreement, the Assembly stopped working on the Thirty-Nine Articles of the Church of England and began to form a new plan for "a more perfect reformation" of the Churches of England, Scotland, and Ireland.

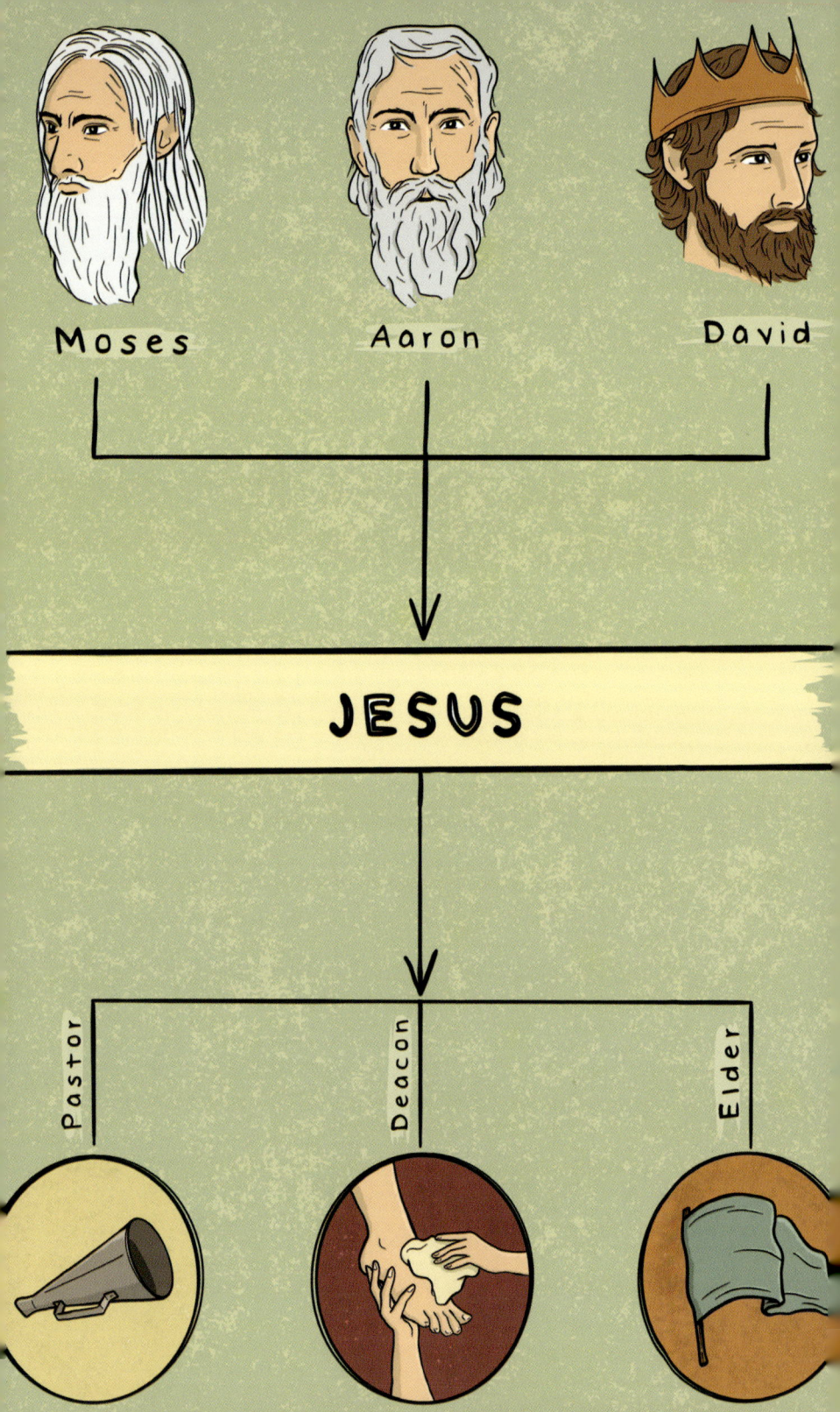

The Westminster Assembly wrote five important documents known as the Westminster Standards. In the Form of Presbyterial Church Government, the Assembly showed how the church should be organized and how new ministers should be set apart for their task.

The government of God's kingdom rests on the shoulders of Jesus Christ. He rules over all creation and is the only head of the church (Eph. 1:22; 5:23). When Jesus left this earth to return to heaven, He appointed officers to care for His flock. Pastors preach God's Word, lead the church in public worship, and shepherd the flock. Teachers are ministers who devote their time to teaching in seminaries and churches. Elders, together with the pastors, rule in the church and care for her members. Deacons use the resources of the church to help the poor.

Members of the Assembly did not all agree on church government. The Episcopalians strove for bishops, individual men ruling over the churches, each in a given district. The Independents argued for the power of each congregation to govern itself, free from any external control. The Erastians wanted to subject the church to the control of the state. Finally, the Presbyterians believed that councils or assemblies of elders should govern local churches, and when the pastors and elders from several churches met together they could make decisions for all their churches. Most members of the Westminster Assembly were Presbyterians, and they taught that view in their Form of Church Government.

The Assembly also wrote the Directory for Public Worship of God, instruction on how the church should worship

- The church comes together on the Lord's day in quiet reverence.
- The pastor reads the Bible while the church listens.
- The church sings psalms to God with grace in their hearts.
- The pastor leads the church in prayer, to adore God, confess sins, thank God for His mercies, ask for the work of the Holy Spirit, intercede for the salvation of the Jews and all nations, and pray for government leaders.

God as He commands in His Word. Even children can understand how to worship in this way.

- The pastor preaches a sermon to explain part of the Bible and apply it by telling people what they must believe and do, comforting those who repent, and warning those who do not.

- The pastor administers baptism and the Lord's Supper.

- The pastor dismisses the congregation with God's blessing or benediction.

- The whole Lord's day is kept as a Sabbath, a holy day of rest.

Of all that the Westminster Assembly wrote, most famous is the Westminster Confession of Faith. A church uses a confession to declare what it believes and teaches. The Bible is the source for all Christian faith, but it is not enough for us to say, "We believe the Bible." Many people claim to believe the Bible while denying what it teaches or disobeying its commands. The Westminster Confession sums up the teaching of God's Word on thirty-three topics: the Holy Scriptures, God, His eternal decree, creation, and providence; human sin, God's covenant, Christ's work as Mediator, humanity's free will; effectual calling, justification, adoption, sanctification, faith, repentance, good works, perseverance, assurance; God's law, Christian liberty, worship and the Sabbath day; oaths and vows, human government, marriage, church, the communion of saints, sacraments, baptism, the Lord's Supper, church censures and councils; death, resurrection, and the last judgment.

The divines at the Westminster Assembly wanted to teach people the doctrines of the church. To do that, they wrote catechisms, little books of questions and answers. One is the Westminster Larger Catechism, which contains 196 questions with detailed answers and proof texts from the Bible.

For example, did you ever wonder what it means to pray "in Jesus's name"? The Larger Catechism says, "To pray in the name of Christ is, in obedience to His command, and in confidence on His promises, to ask mercy for His sake; not by bare mentioning of His name, but by drawing our encouragement to pray, and our boldness, strength, and hope of acceptance in prayer, from Christ and His mediation" (Q. 180). "Mediation" means the work Christ does in coming between God and sinners to bring them together, so that they can pray to God, who is pleased to hear and answer them.

The Westminster Assembly divines especially wanted young people and children to learn what the Bible teaches. Therefore, they wrote the Westminster Shorter Catechism to give simpler answers to 107 questions.

Many people ask, "Why am I here? What is the meaning of life?" The Shorter Catechism says that our main purpose ("man's chief end") is "to glorify God, and to enjoy Him forever" (Q. 1).

People also ask, "What is God?" That is, what kind of being is He, and what is His character? Now that's a deep question! But the catechism again helps us with a short, clear answer: "God is a Spirit, infinite, eternal, and unchangeable, in His being, wisdom, power, holiness, justice, goodness, and truth" (Q. 4).

This catechism is very good for memorizing so that children (and adults) can understand the truths of the Bible in a simple way and explain them to others.

By 1648 the Westminster Assembly had finished its work on the confession and catechisms. A year later, most of its ministers had gone home, though some remained until 1653 to examine men who wanted to become ministers. In the 1650s and 1660s, however, England went through great changes in its civil government. The Westminster Confession and its catechisms never found a lasting place in the Church of England. But they were approved and adopted by the General Assembly of the Church of Scotland; by English Presbyterians; and with some changes, by English Congregationalists and Baptists. From Scotland and England, they were carried to many other parts of the world by immigrants to the United States, Canada, and elsewhere. With the Bible in one hand and the Westminster Standards in the other, faithful Christians laid the foundations of Presbyterian and Reformed churches in many lands and earnestly contended for "the faith which was once delivered to the saints."

NOTE TO PARENTS

The English Reformation is a tumultuous story of victory and defeat. The restoration of Charles II to the throne (1660) and the Act of Uniformity (1662) led to the widespread persecution of Puritans in England and Presbyterians in Scotland. In 1688 England, fearful of a return to Roman Catholicism, requested the help of William of Orange from the Netherlands, who was married to Charles's niece Mary. The Glorious Revolution brought William and Mary to the united throne of the three kingdoms of England, Scotland, and Ireland. In 1689 religious toleration was granted to all English Protestants.

The Puritan quest for reformation and the work of the Westminster Assembly should encourage us to take our place in the army of God and "contend for the faith once delivered to the saints." This is a battle fought and won by the power of truth, prayer, love, and holiness, and a willingness to suffer unto death.

Until the Lord comes again, the church in the world must be the church militant, the church at war. Believers in every generation take their place in God's army. We put on the same armor worn by saints of old. We wield the same weapon, the gospel of Jesus Christ. And we fight to honor our heritage and leave a legacy for future generations.

Our fight will be different from those in earlier generations. The particular truths being contested or the practices called into question may differ. But complacency signals danger. Let us, in the words of the Solemn League and Covenant, "endeavor for ourselves and all others under our power and charge, both in public and private, in all duties we owe to God and man, to amend our lives and each one go before another in the example of a real reformation."

For further reading on the history and theology of the English Reformation and the Westminster Assembly, see William Beveridge, *A Short History of the Westminster Assembly*, originally printed in 1904 and now edited by Ligon Duncan. For the Westminster Standards in one volume, see *The Westminster Confession* (Edinburgh: Banner of Truth Trust, 2018).